FALL COLOURS
across North America

ANTHONY EATON COOK

FOREWORD BY ART WOLFE   ESSAY BY ANN ZWINGER

whitecap

Evening sunlight on Wonder Lake, Denali National Park and Preserve, Alaska.

To my children, Sara and Courtney,
and my niece and nephew, Heather and Brandon,
for the joy they bring to my world.
I hope they find happiness and reward
in our natural heritage.

◆

To my wife, Sandy, who has shared
with me her enthusiasm and blessed my life with
happiness, companionship, and encouragement.

◆

To Art Wolfe, whose devotion to his work
and the preservation of the natural world
has greatly inspired me.

ACKNOWLEDGMENTS

I would like to thank the following people for their
encouragement and support that helped make this book possible:
Robert and Birgit Bateman, Pat and Rosemarie Keough,
Doug Pfeiffer, Tim Frew, Elizabeth Watson, Ellen Wheat,
Jean Bond-Slaughter, Heather Doornink, Heather Lang-Runtz,
Ray Pfortner, Bruce Klein, and Ted Grant.

◆

I would like to acknowledge my use of Fujichrome Velvia film
to take the photographs for this book.

CONTENTS

Title page: A STORM SETTLES OVER ALGONQUIN
PEAK AS SUNLIGHT STREAKS ACROSS THE BASE OF
MOUNT JO, ADIRONDACK PARK, NEW YORK.
Pages 4-5: A FORESTED LANDSCAPE, MERSEY RIVER,
KEJIMKUJIK NATIONAL PARK, NOVA SCOTIA.

Silvery aspen trunks and golden foliage reach toward an azure sky, Turner Valley, Alberta.

A professional photographer for over twenty-five years, I have traveled the world. As my work has evolved, I have captured a great variety of subjects on film, everything from wildlife to sweeping landscapes to indigenous cultures. Throughout those years, my formal training not in photography (actually I have none) but in painting has guided and shaped my images. The classical lessons of form, color, texture, and composition have influenced my artistic vision of the splendors of the natural world.

Whatever the subject, I draw on these lessons in my work. In my book, *Light on the Land*, the quality of light constituted in my mind "the defining moment" of composition. In *Migrations*, form, color, and texture became tools to convey biology. In *The Living Wild*, poignant images of animals in their natural habitats can be appreciated as much for how they are presented—within their environment, where light, form, and pattern all come together—as for what they represent, namely animals in peril.

For me, capturing that defining moment on film, whether the subject is a lioness in Kenya or a desertscape in Mongolia or a tribal dancer in Papua, New Guinea, is my means of conveying experience and expressing emotion. It is how I try to make a difference, to enlist support and action—on behalf of the natural world—from those who see my images. It is how I try to give back to the natural world.

In Anthony Cook's photographs I sense a kindred spirit. In his images I see the same attention to the vignettes of a scene, the same exacting approach to capturing a moment in time at its purest and simplest. Anthony's images are defined by his use of light and by his carefully crafted composition. His

🌿 COUGAR, LOS PADRES NATIONAL FOREST,
VENTURA COUNTY, CALIFORNIA.

photographs attest to his care and dedication, to the countless hours spent long before the shutter is ever fired.

Anthony has crisscrossed North America for more than four years to capture the images of fall color that you see in the following pages. Even more incredible is that in the process, he used only two hundred rolls of film: a tremendous amount of patience and resolve goes into each and every photograph he takes. Anthony once climbed a hundred-and-fifty-foot hemlock tree every day for two months to record a nesting pair of great blue herons in a nearby treetop. For this book, he hiked up one mountain ten times over eight days until just the right light fell onto an adjacent peak. On a typical day of shooting, Anthony rarely photographs more than a few subjects, as he looks for perfection.

I know Anthony well. I believe that his approach to photography and his images reflects three primary influences in his life.

First, his longtime interest in art and especially painting gives his work a painterly quality. His emphasis on the abstract in every composition and his striving to find the dynamic quality of every subject reflect how steeped he is in the arts. These directions set him apart from many of the photographers who document the natural world.

Second, Anthony's friendship with Canadian wildlife painter Robert Bateman has enhanced his sensitivity to and sensibility for all things wild. Robert has been a mentor to Anthony, helping to refine his vision.

Finally, Anthony has a strong conservation ethic, which he shares with Robert and also has derived from experiences close to home. He has used his images and his books to foster conservation of the natural world. Wilderness areas, both within his home state and farther afield, have found in him not just a worthy protector but also an impassioned advocate.

My hat is off to Anthony Cook, for his hard work, his focus, his message, and his achievement.

Art Wolfe
Seattle, Washington

✿ IN THE LATE AUTUMN CHILL, WISPS OF MORNING MIST RISE FROM A WETLAND, BERKSHIRE MOUNTAINS, MASSACHUSETTS.

10 ❧ Birch and aspen fill the boreal forest on the north shore of Lake Superior, Split Rock Lighthouse State Park, Minnesota.

❧ At sunset, golden light reflects along sandstone ridges formed by the ceaseless pounding of waves, Pictured Rocks National Lakeshore, Michigan.

Of all the seasons, autumn is perhaps the most beautiful. She tantalizes us with her ever-changing moods, and we respond to the dance, never certain whether the next day will bring sunshine or showers. On some days the skies forebode snow or rain showers, the result of cold fronts drawing the fury of bitter arctic blasts southward. From experience we search the heavens for the sight of brilliant shafts of sunlight breaking through the dark skies and streaking over the glittering landscape. On other days the autumn sun is surprisingly warm, thanks to unexpected high-pressure fronts—and we are reminded of endless summer days.

As those hazy, warm days become a distant memory, the greens of summer have already begun to fade—a prelude to what I consider the landscape's finest hour. From greens to vibrant colors, the gradual change in foliage hues catches us off guard. Suddenly, we are assaulted by a countryside that pulsates in an exquisite melody of yellow, scarlet, gold, and blue. Then in no time at all, autumn tightens her grip on the landscape. The brilliant colors begin to pale, trees drop their leaves as winter's chill approaches, the days grow ever shorter, and intense arctic winds and sudden snow squalls send squirrels into hyperactivity as they cache their harvest of winter food, and bears rush into feeding frenzies to fatten up before hibernating.

Autumn's multicolored tapestry provides richly inspiring photographic opportunities. From morning to evening, the landscape is transfigured in count-less ways. I have spent many an idyllic afternoon stretched out on a forest floor newly covered with a carpet of fallen leaves, waiting for the evening light to do its magic. As the shadows deepen, I have found myself drawn toward the

JEFFREY PINE CONES AND QUAKING ASPEN
LEAVES, LECONTE CANYON, INYO NATIONAL
FOREST, CALIFORNIA.

ascending branches, where autumnal colors and creeping vines blend into abstract shapes. The harmony of these elements is often enhanced by fog and mist, hue and tone.

The challenge I had set for myself in creating this book—to capture on film the dramatic performance of fall foliage across North America—was a wondrous adventure. Day after day for four autumns, in sun, wind, snow, and rain, I trekked across the continent. My daily sojourns took me through remote areas, from the Alaska tundra and the rugged Yukon wilderness in the Far North to the bald cypress swamps of Louisiana in the south. I traveled through seven Canadian provinces and twenty-eight states in America, on foot, by car, and plane.

With each part of my journey, Nature drew me into her spell. Alone and far from civilization, with only the sound of the wind-rustled leaves as my companion, I felt a kinship with the natural world. It was my kind of activity: working alone, avoiding the distraction of joint decisions, having no one to witness my trials until only the satisfying is accomplished. Was this the intimacy, the primal wisdom that mankind and Nature have shared through most of human history? I believe so.

This solitary adventure came with its own set of challenges, physical and otherwise. Always questing to equal my expectation—to capture a unique moment in autumnal display—I found myself returning again and again to the same spot, having not achieved my vision for that photograph. At Zion National Park in Utah, for example, I learned that the vine maples growing high up on the canyon assume their fall garb far earlier than the cottonwoods on the valley floor. Elsewhere in the nearby mountains of Colorado, the aspens have already discarded their yellow threads. Heavy snow as a result of strong Pacific storm patterns impeded my progress while photographing in the Mount Baker and Alpine Lakes wilderness areas of Washington State. Several times weather and the unpredictability of the fall foliage in the Pacific Northwest played havoc with my travel plans. I won't soon forget the terror I felt when blasts of turbulent mountain air tore wickedly at our small floatplane, as we twisted above the high Nahanni River plateau in Canada's Northwest Territories

MARY ANN FALLS, CAPE BRETON HIGHLANDS NATIONAL PARK, NOVA SCOTIA.

❧ Birch leaves caught in a mountain stream, Great Smoky Mountains National Park, Tennessee.

while photographing mountain sheep. Many times I was indeed at the mercy of nature!

Nor will I forget how elated I was when I finally captured an image that had eluded me many times. In the Adirondack Mountains of New York, I spent eight invigorating days hiking up a boulder-strewn trail to the top of Mount Jo. But each time I reached the pinnacle, the scene pictured in my mind's eye failed to materialize. On my tenth climb through the cold, damp air, I was rewarded. Before me sprawled the mountainous landscape dressed in fall splendor, the small lake below barely discernible beneath a slowly lifting fog mass. A storm approaching from the west darkened the mountains, as the only beam of sunlight to be seen that day streaked across the foreground from the east, lighting the brilliant foliage beneath me.

I will remember vividly the unusual warmth of an early September morning, as I lay hidden in the brush with my camera focused on a Denali grizzly bear as it grazed on low-bush blueberries. I could hear the distant calls of whooping cranes as they circled far above, riding the thermals that would take them over the Alaska mountain ranges and on their way to a southerly destination. Nor will I easily forget the sudden chill that settled on me as the giant bear lurched swiftly from a dense thicket of blueberry bushes toward me.

As humankind has become more civilized, we have distanced ourselves from nature. Each passing autumn season brings renewed evidence that all living things on Earth are bound together in a complex and fragile interrelationship. The miracle that is the cycle of life and death on Earth begins with the fresh green colors of spring and ends with autumn's stunning splash of many colors.

What a grand experience!

Anthony E. Cook

Anthony E. Cook
Cook Forest, Pennsylvania

▲▲ Grizzly bear feeding, Kluane National Park, Yukon Territory. ▲ Red bearberry, Denali National Park and Preserve, Alaska.

18 ❧ September snow is common high in the Wenatchee Mountains overlooking the Cle Elum River valley, Alpine Lakes Wilderness, Washington.

❧ SUMMER CHANGES QUICKLY INTO AUTUMN'S SPLENDOR AT HIGH ELEVATIONS, CLINGMANS DOME, GREAT SMOKY MOUNTAINS NATIONAL PARK, NORTH CAROLINA.

FALL COLORS
Gifts of Glory

Fall colors are like the bouquet a magician pulls out of his sleeve and presents with a flourish to an expectant and amazed audience—a bouquet of resonant crimsons and russets, opulent oranges and glorious golds, lapis blues and amethysts. They materialize like magic where the week before there had been only green. In a wide swath across the northern states and southern Canada, masses of magnificent maples and operatic oaks and beeches emblazon the hillsides. Scrub oaks puddle the foothills with molten bronze. Cottonwoods trace creek beds in golden serpentines like a topographical map upon which watercourses are limned in saffron instead of blue. Larches turn into pyramids of topaz. Bigleaf maples pave the ground of the Northwest with huge amber leaves beneath the soaring scarlet of vine maples. Elm leaves slither down to lurk like goldfish in the grass. Along the Blue Ridge Parkway and in the Adirondacks drivers pack the roads to canonize the miles of glorious color, the dazzling spectrum of colors that led Edna St. Vincent Millay to write of these woods, these autumn days, that almost cry with color.

Such bombastic bursts of color appear predominantly in North America between latitudes 30 and 70 degrees north, where temperate deciduous forests thrive, the forests that present this yearly rise of color. Here, in the United States and up into Canada, when trees do their thing, they wrap themselves in gaudy shifts of color, do a naughty Charleston and drink champagne on Monday

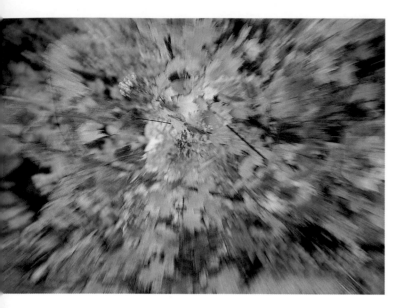

morning. Here flourish the trees that produce autumns with an attitude, jazzy brilliant blazes of color that can time a year, shape a conversation, call forth remembrances laced with superlatives.

I grew up in Indiana where fall blazed in copses, on hillsides, beside streams, along roads. In my childhood, fall was a marked and major event. Every year. Remarked and remarkable. In my memory, I hold dear the fall colors of Indiana, splendid stretches of glorious color, placed by chance and botanical necessity. I was a child not much given to philosophical speculation, but the fact that my family, which didn't do much traveling, would drive a hundred miles to see trees in autumn foliage made a big impression. I got the message even then that these trees, these colors, these smells and sounds, these ceremonies of passage, were important. Even then I must have sensed that they were annual reminders, stabilizers, balancers, that spoke simply and evenly about getting prepared for winter.

But I was blissfully ignorant that this display depended upon the wide swaths of temperate forests, the development of which is a fairly recent event in geologic history, becoming established around sixty-six million years ago when the global climate cooled. The erstwhile prevailing hot, damp equatorial climate shifted to a cooler and drier climate increasingly marked with seasonal changes that were strongly affected by latitude, and deciduous trees evolved from their evergreen ancestors of the tropical rainforest. Some trees could not adapt and went extinct, while others could and, in time, dominated the new temperate forests.

Alternating glacial and interglacial periods of the last two million years forced the trees to constantly adjust in order to survive and flourish—as they have in North America. Trees that were able to disperse their seeds widely were most successful in colonizing new areas and, as a consequence, the deciduous forests migrated back and forth to keep within their ecological parameters. Where they grow today is a result of their continuing adaptation to current climatic patterns.

The temperate forest needs a temperate climate in which to flourish: cool springs, warm summers, cool falls, cold winters, and days of changing length—

❧ Blue Ridge Mountains, Jackson County, North Carolina.

the gift of seasons Prometheus swore he had given humans. The new temperate regime of long cold winters with short days meant that many species of trees in the temperate forest had to cope with too little daylight to make sufficient food all year long, and their leaves were often in danger of freezing; with winters too long and summers too short, thin-leafed trees had insufficient time and temperature to leaf out and set seed. As a consequence, most trees are wind-pollinated, independent of insects. The only trees that can survive the most stringent conditions at the outer limits are those not bound by a yearly cycle of leafing, trees with leaves narrowed into needles and coated with a protective resin, imbued with a sap that does not freeze at zero degrees Centigrade.

Temperate forest trees solved the climate challenge by becoming deciduous. Just as many animals go into hibernation to survive the inimical season, deciduous trees go dormant by reducing leaf inventory and shutting down food production. Despite the amount of energy necessary to make a new crop of leaves every year, not having leaves in the winter spares a tree from being killed by below-freezing temperatures. In preparation for dropping its leaves, the connection between the leaf and the tree's circulatory system becomes blocked, as a corklike abscission layer forms at the base of the leaf petiole. The abscission layer softens, the attachment of leaf to twig weakens, and the break-down of green chlorophyll begins.

In the smudged yellow along the veins of an oak leaf, I follow the sturdy thread lines of veins that served as conduits, crossing dots of remaining green. Holding it against a strong light I can almost sense the pulsing of tiny pools of chlorophyll between the veins. For a split second I tune into, in the most intimate way, the pulse of life, the normal cycle of greening up and shutting down. Then the pigments in the leaf, hidden by chlorophyll in the summer, become visible: red anthocyanins, yellow carotenes, and xanthophylls. That pragmatic act of the tree results in a totally unexpected aesthetic effect: magnificent fall colors.

Red in all its variations emblazons trees and shrubs in hues varied and rich: alizarin oaks, Venetian scarlet, richer words than plain old terse three-letter "red." The purveyors range through hemoglobin red sumac, garnet currants, mahogany red wild rose leaves surrounding shiny, strawberry red rose hips,

26   Vine maple thicket, Alpine Lakes Wilderness, Washington.

a carnelian ruffle around the twin black berries of a mountain honeysuckle, deep rose wild dogwood leaves and stems, ruddy tupelo and ruby swamp maples around Walden Pond, cinnabar red cranberries in the Pine Barrens, and vermillion blueberry leaves spread across an Alaska slope. Seek red and ye shall find it.

A maple leaf appears red because the leaf absorbs light from the blue and green range of the spectrum, and reflects what we perceive as red. We see green when the shortwave red end of the spectrum is absorbed. No wonder the complexities and physics of perceived color get lost in the familiar imagery of Jack Frost, paint pot in hand, gleefully coating the leaves or, in some instances, spilling a whole bucket of color over a hillside.

FROSTED FERNS AND VINE MAPLE LEAVES, ALPINE LAKES WILDERNESS, WASHINGTON.

Reds come from chemicals called anthocyanins, substances that produce the reds of beets and maple leaves, and the purples and magentas of red cabbages and onions. Ironically, for all their showiness, these stunning fall colors appear to have little practical use for the tree—attracting no pollinator, providing no camouflage, sending no clear message—except to human eyes, to which they carry a message of change and glory.

After the reds come the oranges and yellows: brilliant orange of bittersweet, or the gilded yellow of aspen in full regalia, including a few orange clumps with leaves like new pennies. These leaves are yellow because the most prevalent pigments hidden in the leaf are the yellow xanthophylls and carotenes, the chemicals that also make carrots orange.

At this time of year when color is so upstage, I feel a need to identify individual hues, to tap into the rich vocabulary of colors, to distinguish precisely the shade that separates yellow larch from yellow maple, to differentiate "gamboges" from "cadmium." The dictionary does give me much help; it tells me that gamboge is "a strong yellow that is redder and less strong than yolk yellow or light chrome yellow," and cadmium yellow is "a strong orange that is yellower and paler than pumpkin, yellower, less strong, and slightly lighter than cadmium orange, and yellower and paler than mandarin orange," and gives synonyms of "daffodil," "nasturtium," and "Orient yellow."

Better than the dictionary, if you want to know what color you're enjoying, you can walk into any art store and consult the color chart for a full box of colored pencils or watercolor pigments. There are all those luscious words for colors you always wanted to know but never took time to ask about: madder and ultramarine, burnt sienna and banana yellow, cobalt blue and Tyrian purple. The more scientifically minded can consult Mr. Munsell's *Book of Color*, a thorough array of every hue and tone possible, by which one can calculate not only hue but also value and chroma. Or explore the Tristmulus System, which involves matching an unfamiliar color with standard samples of red, green, and blue, arranged in a chromaticity diagram. There may be no proper names for some colors, and they simply lodge in memory as a little south of lemon yellow, a little west of daffodil, and a little deeper than butter.

🍂 AUTUMN LEAVES ARE TRAPPED IN THE WHIRLPOOL OF A WOODLAND STREAM, MOUNT MITCHELL STATE PARK, NORTH CAROLINA.

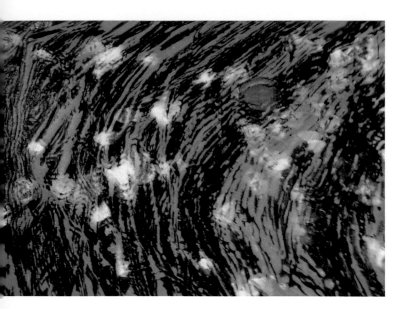

In the High Country of Colorado where I live, falls are yellow, and they begin in late August when the dogbane leaves turn butterscotch, weeks before any other plant has even considered preparing itself for winter. Dogbane is not the drop-dead kind of plant one would expect to be a harbinger of a whole change in season; it's only a foot or so high, with small dangling, bell-like flowers and languid leaves, easily overlooked. But when the leaves glow that particular soft and resonant buttery-brown yellow, I hear in my ears the haunting lines and mournful long "O" sounds of Paul Verlaine's *Chanson de L'Automne*, about the sobbing violins of autumn:

> *des sanglots longs*
> *des violons*
> *de l'automne*

I feel in my own heart the sadness of the coming closure, and I grieve that neither piety nor wit will change one yellowing leaf back to green again.

Six weeks later the aspen leaves quiver like nuggets of gold in a stream of sonorous green spruce and pine and Douglas fir. Aspens form the northernmost fringe of trees, the upper reaches of deciduous trees, the outliers before conifers predominate. The aspen's success depends on a method of reproduction very different from most deciduous trees. They grow in clones, connected underground, able to send up new shoots from underground ramets without having to go through the hazards of sprouting seeds each year. Each clone acts as a huge, undivided tree, with its own time of flushing spring leaves, of turning yellow, and its own shade of yellow that can vary from lemon to salmon to an occasional sandy red, the color change defining the margins of each clone. The contrasting colors depend on variations in soil chemistry, slope exposure, genetic makeup, and a grab bag of inexplicables that bless trees, growing so closely that their upper branches may touch, with smartly different colors.

Because green generally disappears, we don't much associate green with fall colors, but without that color many of the displays would be less dramatic. It's that formidable, somber, thick, dark green that forms a background for colored

🍂 FALLING LEAVES, CONCENTRIC RINGS, RIPPLED WATER, BAXTER STATE PARK, MAINE.

🦅 A SEA GULL RISES WITH A FLURRY OF BEATING
WINGS IN AUTUMN REFLECTIONS, ACADIA
NATIONAL PARK, MAINE.

trees, especially aspen—there's even a color termed "forest green" that calls to mind that particular dark and sturdy color of conifers, and the cool quality of green sets off the blazing colors of leaves.

Big red and gold trees get all the splashy PR. But being too enamored of the big continents of color on the hillsides in a green sea, we miss the smaller, more subtle changes—lack the focus that discerns the exquisite color patterns in a fine tapestry, or the tatting on the fallen, lace-edged handkerchiefs of yarrow or the last pearly everlasting. Who can imagine fall without fat orange pumpkins? While you watch, summer's bluebells phase from a tender sky blue to an intense lapis lazuli as the days shorten. The late asters that last week were lavender are, a week later, a deep and glowing Tyrian purple. And we miss most of the short-wave end of the spectrum that appears in smaller portions, like the Concord grapes hanging in obese clusters, or fat and frosted lapis blueberries, or in the Northwest, big purple boletus mushrooms bursting through the forest duff.

With all the big and brazen colors it's easy to miss the more minikin shifts and the changes played pianissimo. In our passionate preference for things in living, over-vivid color rather than black and white and sepia tints, we miss the exquisitely subtle browns and bronzes, the brass and henna, the cinnamons, siennas, and burnt umbers, that fill the meadows. Grasses turn distinctive colors just as trees do, but they require a more discriminating eye. Little bluestem switches to rose, one of those misnomers nature is heir to. Timothy becomes a straw-colored metronome, ticking away the season. Nodding brome becomes immortalized in bronze. One meadow I know lies so that it becomes backlit by late afternoon sun; then what was a tan, fairly pedestrian sweep of dried grasses suddenly becomes a raging strawberry blond, a color that the elderly Renoir, brush strapped to his arthritic arm, brushed on with panache for his fleshy nudes. The meadow incandesces as it catches flame in the light—vital, glowing, saturated with enough color to hold back the cold.

Fall color may even be absence of color, noncolor: white baneberries look like porcelain beads arrayed on a stalk, and snowberries like a smattering of hail in the woods. The last white cabbage butterflies still optimistically patrol for a late mustard plant on which to lay eggs. Clematis seed heads, crimped

Brightly lit leaves above a stream create colorful patterns, East Branch Ausable River, New York.

filaments of white, tumble over fences and boulders. Observe the assurance of continuity in fireweed seeds, continuity assured in a white wisp of immortality. And don't miss the most exquisite of them all, cool white arctic gentian, nestled in the thin coppery stems of the sedge with which it grows in the alpine tundra.

Discovering where to go to find the glorious changes of fall takes time. But that recognition brings with it pleasure, evokes the memory of past autumns, gives us the chance to compare, opine, reminisce. Verbalizing makes the experience aural, organizes it into memory, causes it to be more true and more lasting. Writing things down makes them real, congeals them in memory, provides a reference. That's why people keep journals. There may be as much discussion about the change of fall colors as there is of the weather. And people do not follow Mark Twain's dictum, people *do* something about it: they get out in droves to see it, clotting the back roads and inhaling the glory, and have been doing so for decades. Each new fall invites comparisons with past falls, each of which may be remembered separately with the contemplative precision of an oenophile contemplating a vintage noir. We retain surprisingly acute memories of timing and depth of color and specific places and moments. Each of us, in one way or another, is an aficionado of fall colors.

That unparalleled chronicler of autumn colors, Henry David Thoreau, ruminated in his journal in the fall of 1853 how fine it would be "to get a specimen leaf from each changing tree and shrub and plant in autumn, in September and October, when it had got its brightest characteristic color, the intermediate ripeness in its transition from the green to the russet or brown state, outline and copy its color exactly with paint in a book—a book which should be a memorial of October, to be entitled October Hues or Autumnal Tints . . . What a memento such a book would be, beginning with the earliest reddening of the leaves, woodbine and ivy, etc. etc. . . . down to the latest oaks!" How much one would learn by doing just that! Not only the color but the way gingko veins splay out from the stem like miniature fans; how maple leaves order their vascular system; how the flattened stem of an aspen leaf engenders the giddy flutter of the leaves.

The big, easily seen colors of hillside trees may gradually attune us to others

◀ EARLY SNOW FALLS IN A YOUNG DECIDUOUS FOREST, CUYAHOGA VALLEY NATIONAL RECREATION AREA, OHIO.

▲ UPPER ROCK CREEK, INYO NATIONAL FOREST, CALIFORNIA.

❧ ANCIENT FLORA SPECIES PROVIDE A TIMELESS REMNANT OF THE ICE AGE, GREAT SMOKY MOUNTAINS NATIONAL PARK, TENNESSEE.

more delicately endowed and their accompanying subtle changes: red stains along the veins of a yellow maple leaf, the brassy orange or amber cap of a fall russula, the sedge stem copper, the ptarmigan and snowshoe hare turning white in preparation for snow, the silence of those who go underground, the nostalgic aroma of burning leaves twining upward in gray smoke wisps, the almost imperceptible touch of a featherweight leaf commanding its own cylinder of air as it wafts its boustrophedon path downward. And the concomitant sounds: the clatter and whisper of leaves, the susurrus and sibilance of meadow grasses, the stridulation and rasp of drying rushes. And the thick odors of fall: the sweet, almost cloying smell of drying aspen leaves, the ineffable scent of musty mushrooms, the sharp smoky savor of burning leaves.

I invite whosoever reads these pages to go forth and collect a dozen new and different colored leaves and press them. Send a red leaf to someone far away. Note the last mourning cloak butterfly scouting out a place to hibernate. Distinguish between the hemoglobin red of sumac leaves and the cardinal red of wild geranium leaves. Pop open a milkweed pod and blow a seed on its way. Recite Helen Hunt Jackson's memorable quatrain about "October's bright blue weather." Rake up a pile of leaves and leap into them like a kid, crumple them in your hand so that they sound like tissue paper wrapping up a present of fall's privileges. Check the sunset, ruddy and luminous, as late light filters through the glinting dust spiraling into the air. Mark the lengthening shadows that, for a few moments, enrich the colors around you, making them resonate in the late hours of the day that parallel the late days of the season.

Watch the grasses gossip and blow. Read Thoreau's *Journals*. Listen to the sounds of crimson and carnelian, the roar of maple, the salmon of salal, the bell-like tinkle of aspen, and the clatter of oak leaves in a coastal sea wind. Honor those players of nature that, by changing their hues, suffuse the meadows and roadsides and forests with rich colors. Privilege these late, shortening days of the year, which juxtapose flaring, blazing colors effulgent against the fawns and grays of a departing year. Honor the glorious, flamboyant fall colors that bespeak gifts of glory, answered expectations, and nature's foresighted and considered preparation for the respite of winter.

▲ In fall, great deciduous forests provide ample duff to the forest floor, Big South Fork National River and Recreation Area, Tennessee.

► Thorofare River, Denali National Park and Preserve, Alaska.

BLUEBERRIES, LOWBUSH CRANBERRIES, AND DWARF WILLOWS OF THE NORTHERN TUNDRA TURN BRILLIANT AUTUMN HUES, DENALI HIGHWAY, ALASKA.

🌿 A COW MOOSE CROSSES THE NORTH END OF WONDER LAKE, DENALI NATIONAL PARK AND PRESERVE, ALASKA.

🌿 THE MOON RISES OVER THE ALASKA RANGE, WHICH IS GLOWING PINK AS THE LINGERING SUNSET DRAPES THE MOUNTAINS, DENALI NATIONAL PARK AND PRESERVE, ALASKA.

🌿 ◄ THE SETTING SUN HIGHLIGHTS WILLOWS AND LOWBUSH CRANBERRIES THAT CIRCLE WONDER LAKE NEAR THE BASE OF MOUNT MCKINLEY, DENALI NATIONAL PARK AND PRESERVE, ALASKA.

▲ CARIBOU FOLLOW ANCIENT MIGRATION ROUTES THROUGH DENALI NATIONAL PARK AND PRESERVE, ALASKA.

45

❧ NOCTURNAL BY NATURE, BEAVERS BECOME ACTIVE NIGHT AND DAY DURING THE FALL TO CACHE SUFFICIENT

FOOD FOR THE WINTER, SOUTH NAHANNI RIVER, NAHANNI NATIONAL PARK, NORTHWEST TERRITORIES.

A BEAVER LODGE STANDS SECURE BEFORE WINTER'S FURY, SIBBESTON RIVER, NORTHWEST TERRITORIES.

🍂 Virginia Falls, South Nahanni River, Northwest Territories.

❧ A discarded moose antler at Little Doctor Lake, Nahanni Range, Northwest Territories.

🌿 ◀ Sunrise in early autumn on the Saint Elias Range along the border between the Yukon Territory and British Columbia.

▲ Snow-covered branches of the Western larch tree, Yoho National Park, British Columbia.

▶ High in the peaks, a sudden snowstorm descends as golden Western larch trees reflect in the turquoise water of a small lake, Yoho National Park, British Columbia.

🌿 ◄ Moraine Lake owes its stunning aquamarine color to pulverized rock particles washed from nearby glaciers, Banff National Park, Alberta.

▲ Shear mountain walls surround a shallow crystal clear lake near Mount Deltaform, Yoho National Park, British Columbia.

56 ❧ Richly colored vine maple leaves are tossed about in a light breeze, North Cascades National Park, Washington.

MAJESTIC MOUNTAINS BENEATH A MANTLE OF SNOW ALONG THE BORDER BETWEEN THE UNITED STATES AND CANADA, MOUNT BAKER WILDERNESS, WASHINGTON.

❧ Deciduous bigleaf maple trees line the banks of Eagle Creek, providing a bright counterpoint to the evergreen vegetation, Columbia River Gorge National Scenic Area, Oregon.

❧ ▲ Luxuriant rain forest dominates the Hoh River Valley, Olympic National Park, Washington.

▶ Delicate vine maples punctuate the verdant coniferous forest, Mount Hood National Forest, Oregon.

▶ ▶ On Eagle Creek, Punchbowl Falls is framed by the lush greens of a dense evergreen forest, Columbia River Gorge National Scenic Area, Oregon.

✿ FOR A BRIEF PERIOD BEFORE DROPPING THEIR NEEDLES IN THE FALL, WESTERN LARCH TURN A GLORIOUS GOLD, SELKIRK MOUNTAINS, IDAHO.

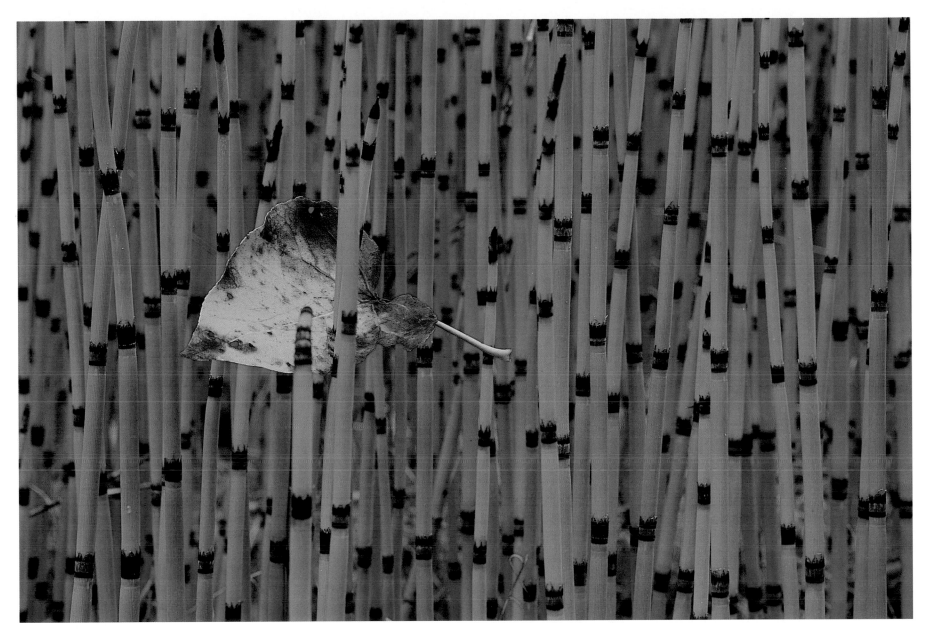

A POPLAR LEAF RESTS AMONG GIANT HORSETAILS, WILLAMETTE NATIONAL FOREST, OREGON.

ELOWAH FALLS, COLUMBIA RIVER GORGE NATIONAL SCENIC AREA, OREGON.

❧ A lively mountain stream tumbles precipitously from the Sierra Nevadas, Upper Rock Creek, Inyo National Forest, California.

◄ ORANGE AND YELLOW ASPENS STAND IN SPLENDOR BEFORE THE
WHITE BACKDROP OF THE SIERRA NEVADA, LITTLE LAKES VALLEY,
INYO NATIONAL FOREST, CALIFORNIA.

▲ FOR THIS COYOTE IN JOSHUA TREE NATIONAL PARK, CALIFORNIA,
A BRIEF AUTUMN SEASON BEGINS IN DECEMBER AND LASTS UNTIL
MID-JANUARY.

❧ THE FIRST RAYS OF A BLAZING SUNRISE STRIKE THE WEATHER-SCULPTED HOODOOS OF BRYCE CANYON NATIONAL PARK, UTAH.

❧ TURQUOISE WATER POURS OVER HAVASU FALLS, HAVASUPAI INDIAN RESERVATION, ARIZONA.

◄ Brilliant yellow aspens crown a mountain ridge high above Grand Staircase–Escalante National Monument, Dixie National Forest, Utah.

► Red Rock Crossing, Oak Creek, Arizona.

71

❧ Fremont cottonwoods and gambel oaks thrive along the Virgin
River below steep canyon walls, Zion National Park, Utah.

❧ A Fremont cottonwood stands alone against the backdrop of intricate cross-bedded sandstone, Checkerboard Mesa, Zion National Park, Utah.

BRILLIANT STRIPED
SANDSTONE REFLECTS THE
AZURE SKY IN THE
NARROWS OF THE VIRGIN
RIVER CANYON, ZION
NATIONAL PARK, UTAH.

❧ ▲ An aspen leaf is encapsulated in ice that edges a misty waterfall
near Weller Lake, White River National Forest, Colorado.
▶ Frigid winds sweep light new snow over high-country ridges,
Rocky Mountain National Park, Colorado.

❧ SNEFFELS RANGE, SAN JUAN
MOUNTAINS, COLORADO.

78

❧ MAPLE LEAVES CLENCH IN FROZEN REPOSE, ROCKY MOUNTAIN NATIONAL PARK, COLORADO.

❧ A SUN-DAPPLED ASPEN GROVE IS SUFFUSED WITH THE SOFT GLOW OF REFLECTED GOLDEN LIGHT, KEBLER PASS, GUNNISON NATIONAL FOREST, COLORADO.

MAROON LAKE,
MAROON BELLS—
SNOWMASS WILDERNESS
AREA, COLORADO.

83

High bluffs on Oberg Mountain in the Sawtooth Range provide a grand view of the Lake Superior highlands, Superior National Forest, Minnesota.

FLOATING SUGAR MAPLE LEAVES REFLECT PATCHES OF LIGHT, OTTAWA NATIONAL FOREST, MICHIGAN.

BOND FALLS, UPPER PENINSULA, MICHIGAN.

88 ❧ WINDBLOWN TREE TRUNKS AND BRANCHES CREATE A LUSH, IMPRESSIONISTIC PALETTE OF FALL FOLIAGE, CHEQUAMEGON NATIONAL FOREST, WISCONSIN.

🍂 AUTUMN'S PASSING HUES ARE REFLECTED IN A REMOTE LAKE, SUPERIOR NATIONAL FOREST, MINNESOTA.

❧ Tannic acid from conifers growing along the stream foams in swirling, turbulent water, Temperance River State Park, Minnesota.

❧ CHAPEL FALLS, PICTURED ROCKS NATIONAL LAKESHORE, MICHIGAN.

❧ EARLY MORNING MIST RISES ON HEART LAKE,
ADIRONDACK PARK, NEW YORK.

92

94 ❧ The scarlet of maple leaves dominates the varied vegetation along the Blue Ridge Parkway, Boone, North Carolina.

 BLUE RIDGE ESCARPMENT, MOUNTAIN BRIDGE WILDERNESS, SOUTH CAROLINA.

❧ YELLOW BRANCH FALLS, OCONEE STATE PARK, SOUTH CAROLINA.

LINVILLE FALLS, LINVILLE GORGE WILDERNESS AREA, NORTH CAROLINA.

❧ WESTON LAKE, CONGAREE SWAMP NATIONAL MONUMENT, SOUTH CAROLINA.

❧ SOARING TULIP TREES, GREAT SMOKY MOUNTAINS NATIONAL PARK, TENNESSEE.

❧ BALD CYPRESS TREES AND CYPRESS ROOTS, CALLED KNEES, ARE AN INTEGRAL PART OF A PRISTINE SWAMP ENVIRONMENT, CYPRESS GARDENS, SOUTH CAROLINA.

🌿 Grand bald cypress trees reach for the sun, Cypress Gardens, South Carolina.

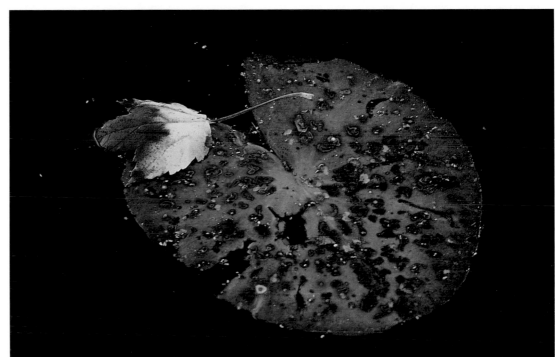

✿ ◄ A MULTIHUED WETLAND SUNRISE PERVADES ACADIA

WILDLIFE MANAGEMENT AREA, RHODE ISLAND.

▲ A RED MAPLE LEAF RESTS ON A LILY PAD, DELAWARE

WATER GAP, PENNSYLVANIA.

WETLANDS LIKE BUZZARD SWAMP IN THE ALLEGHENY NATIONAL FOREST, PENNSYLVANIA, PROVIDE WELCOME REFUGE FOR MIGRATORY WATERFOWL.

✢ STATELY SYCAMORE TREES ANCHOR THE SOIL OF A SMALL ISLAND NESTLED AMONG THE ROCKS OF THE YOUGHIOGHENY RIVER, PENNSYLVANIA.

❧ THE FIRST BRILLIANT RAYS OF THE RISING SUN SWEEP ACROSS THE SUGAR MAPLE CANOPY, COOK FOREST PARK, PENNSYLVANIA.

❧ Fog rises from the New River Valley, New River Gorge National River, West Virginia.

108 ❧ A GRAND OLD CHESTNUT OAK WINDS ITS WAY TOWARD THE SKY, COOPERS ROCK STATE FOREST, WEST VIRGINIA.

✿ BRILLIANT MOUNTAIN RIDGES, GREEN MOUNTAINS, VERMONT.

110 ❧ QUARTZITE ROCK FORMS THE MASSIVE CLIFFS OF THE SHAWANGUNK MOUNTAINS, NEW YORK.

❧ MOUNT EVERETT STATE RESERVATION, MASSACHUSETTS.

❧ TIGHT CLUSTERS OF WHITE-BARKED PAPER BIRCH ABOUND ALONG THE ANDROSCOGGIN RIVER, WHITE MOUNTAIN NATIONAL FOREST, NEW HAMPSHIRE.

❧ Youghiogheny River, Ohiopyle State Park, Pennsylvania.

A yellow birch stands in contrast to schist, Smugglers Notch State Park, Vermont.

FALL TRANSFORMS THE TOP OF THIS RED MAPLE INTO A PANOPLY OF RED AND GREEN, CUYAHOGA VALLEY NATIONAL RECREATION AREA, OHIO.

✿ THE ELLIS RIVER FLOWS RAPIDLY THROUGH GRANITE SLOPES ON THE VERGE OF A WATERFALL, AS FOG LIFTS FROM THE VALLEY BEYOND, WHITE MOUNTAIN NATIONAL FOREST, NEW HAMPSHIRE.

EASTERN HEMLOCK AND
BLACK CHERRY ARE
BLANKETED WITH FRESH
SNOW, ALLEGHENY NATIONAL
FOREST, PENNSYLVANIA.

A CLOSE-UP VIEW OF YOUNG MAPLE TREES, ACADIA NATIONAL PARK, MAINE.

EARLY FALL ON KANCAMAGUS PASS, NEW HAMPSHIRE.

✗ AGAINST THE RUGGED BLUFFS OF THE NIAGARA ESCARPMENT, AN OLD FENCE LINE REPRESENTS A TRANQUIL WAY OF LIFE THAT IS RAPIDLY DISAPPEARING, ONTARIO, CANADA.

THE DIABLE RIVER, PARC DU MONT-TREMBLANT, QUEBEC.

122 ❧ ▲ Halfway Brook and ▶ Clyburn Brook, Cape Breton Island, Nova Scotia.

◆ Gypsum cliffs reflect morning light, Cape Breton Island, Nova Scotia.

▲ Parasol-topped mushrooms, Parc du Mont-Tremblant, Quebec.

▶ Reindeer moss and blueberries, Broad Cove Mountain, Cape Breton Highlands National Park, Nova Scotia.

Photographs © 2001 by Anthony E. Cook
Text © 2001 by Ann Zwinger
Book compilation © 2001 by Graphic Arts Center Publishing®
An imprint of Graphic Arts Center Publishing Company

This edition published in Canada by Whitecap Books Ltd. by
arrangement with Graphic Arts Center Publishing Company.
President: Charles M. Hopkins
Associate Publisher: Douglas A. Pfeiffer
Editorial Staff: Timothy W. Frew, Ellen Harkins Wheat, Tricia
    Brown, Kathy Matthews, Jean Andrews, Jean Bond-Slaughter
Production Staff: Richard L. Owsiany, Heather Doornink
Designer: Elizabeth Watson
Pre-press services: CTI Group
Printing: Haagen Printing
Binding: Lincoln & Allen Company

For more information, contact
Whitecap Books
351 Lynn Avenue
North Vancouver, BC V7J 2C4

National Library of Canada Cataloguing in Publication Data
    Cook, Anthony E., 1964-
        Fall colours across North America
        ISBN 1-55285-287-3
        1. Fall foliage—North America. 2. Fall foliage—
    North America—Pictorial works. I. Zwinger, Ann. II. Title.
        QK110 .C66 2001   581.4'8'0970222   C2001-910991-1

Printed in the United States of America

The publisher acknowledges the support of the Canada Council
and the Cultural Services Branch of the Government of British
Columbia in making this publication possible. We acknowledge
the financial support of the Government of Canada through the
Book Publishing Industry Development Program for our
publishing activities.

BLACK BROOK, CAPE BRETON HIGHLANDS NATIONAL PARK, NOVA SCOTIA.